BIGFOOT
ENDURING MYSTERIES

KEN KARST

Published by
CREATIVE EDUCATION

P.O. Box 227, Mankato, Minnesota 56002
Creative Education is an imprint of The Creative Company
www.thecreativecompany.us

Design and production by Danny Nanos of Gilbert & Nanos
Art direction by Rita Marshall
Printed in the United States of America

Photographs by Corbis (Antonino Barbagallo, Bettmann, DAVID GRAY/Reuters, David Samuel Robbins),
Getty Images (Colin Keates), iStockphoto (JLFCapture, Roberto A Sanchez), Shutterstock (andreiuc88,
Esteban De Armas, ason, Matthew Benoit, Jaimie Duplass, Daniel Goodchild, Everett Collection, fusebulb,
Im Perfect Lazybones, IrinaK, Eric Isselee, Kellis, val lawless, Claudio Del Luongo, Maxx-Studio, Sergey Mironov,
Bradley Allen Murrell, Ken Nyborg, ollyy, Vadim Petrakov, Olga Popova, somchaij, Denis Tabler, Sergey Uryadnikov,
Steven Wright), SuperStock (Animals Animals, Brandon Hauser/Science Faction, SuperStock)
Series logo illustration by Anne Yvonne Gilbert

Library of Congress Cataloging-in-Publication Data

Karst, Ken.
Bigfoot / Ken Karst.
p. cm. — (Enduring mysteries)
Includes bibliographical references and index.
Summary: An investigative approach to the curious phenomena and mysterious circumstances
surrounding the creature known as Bigfoot, from reported sightings to hoaxes to hard facts.

ISBN 978-1-60818-402-6
1. Sasquatch—Juvenile literature. I. Title.

QL89.2.S2K37 2014

001.944—dc23   2013036076

CCSS: RI.5.1, 2, 3, 6, 8; RH.6-8.4, 5, 6, 7, 8

FIRST EDITION
9 8 7 6 5 4 3 2 1

CREATIVE EDUCATION

Table of Contents

In 1967, Roger Patterson was horseback riding through California's Bluff Creek Canyon with a friend when their horses suddenly reared. Only 60 feet (18.3 m) ahead, squatting along the edge of the creek in bright sunlight, was a dark, furry creature that Patterson was certain was a Bigfoot. Patterson had brought a movie camera with him, because he knew others had reported seeing Bigfoot in that area. But the camera was in a saddlebag, and Patterson had been thrown from his horse. By the time he got the camera and started shooting film, the Bigfoot had stood up and started moving away.

Patterson filmed the Bigfoot walking toward the woods, swinging its long arms with each loping step while looking back at the camera for part of the time. Patterson had only about a minute's worth of film left in his camera, but that minute has been examined even more closely than any Academy Award-winning movie in the past 40 years. Was it clear proof, at last, that the giant, ape-like creatures existed? Or, as some said, was the Bigfoot in Patterson's movie just a person in an ape costume with a funny way of walking? Those answers remain as elusive as Bigfoot itself.

BIGFOOT COUNTRY

If you were a creature that just wanted to be left alone, where would you settle? Some of the wildest and most remote parts of the United States and Canada might appeal to you. Dominated by heavily forested mountains, volcanoes, glaciers, tumbling rivers, and giant redwood trees, the Pacific Northwest can be a good place to hide. Black bears, cougars, and wolves—animals whose secretiveness, size, strength, and skills have made them some of the most honored and feared creatures on Earth—make it their home. Some people believe that the area is also home to another large, elusive creature: Bigfoot, also known as Sasquatch.

No one knows for sure what Bigfoot calls home, because Bigfoot is more mystery than fact. A huge, hairy figure that is said to walk like a human, whistle, smell bad, and leave enormous footprints but little else, Bigfoot has been the subject of stories of the northwestern woods for centuries. But what is it, exactly? Is it an ape? That would make it the only

Oregon's volcanic Mt. Hood (below) and its expansive alpine forests are home to black bears (opposite)—and possibly Bigfoot.

known ape in the Americas. Or is it a different kind of **hominid** that has somehow escaped scientific notice for millions of years? Is it a man, too embarrassed by his immense size, hair-covered body, bad smell, and, of course, big feet, to spend time in polite society? Or is it just a bear?

Those are questions that have pestered researchers and travelers in the western woods for generations. Many people, scientists included, simply dismiss Bigfoot as a **myth**, a creature invented by the imaginations of people who've been in the wilderness either so long they've lost their sense of reality or not long enough to understand what's out there and what's not. Although people have been reporting Bigfoot encounters since the 1800s, and similar creatures appear in American Indian lore from long ago, no one has ever found physical evidence, such as a Bigfoot bone or tooth. Scientists learn about animals from those sorts of **spoor**. Without them, Bigfoot remains a phantom creature whose existence no one can prove.

But what about the footprints? Bigfoot has supposedly left thousands of oversized footprints throughout the woods, and dozens of plaster **casts** of those footprints are stored in colleges, universities, research offices, and the basements of Bigfoot chasers. Using footprints as their starting point, Bigfoot researchers have built a case for the existence of Bigfoot, literally from the ground up.

Two thousand Bigfoot sightings have been documented all over the U.S. and Canada in the past 20 years, with dozens more occurring every year. It's believed that the reported sightings represent only a fraction of the total sightings, because many people who see a Bigfoot keep the story to themselves, out of fear of ridicule. Grover Krantz (1931–2002), an anthropologist at Washington State University and one of the few scholars to give Bigfoot stories serious consideration, estimated there could be 2,000 Bigfoot living in the woods across the northwestern U.S. and southwestern Canada. And sightings of similar creatures have been reported in other countries around the world, where they've been given names such as Yeti, Yowie, Skunk Ape, Alma, and Wildman. Bigfoot itself has reportedly appeared on every continent except Antarctica. The majority of sightings have been in the Pacific Northwest, where American Indian tribes have long told stories of these huge, humanlike yet ape-like beings. Those forest-dwellers called the beings by many names, including "Sesquac" and "Sasehavas." In the 1920s, a Canadian journalist and schoolteacher named J. W. Burns invented the term Sasquatch, which is the name for Bigfoot most often used in Canada.

In 2013, New York's Daily News reported that researchers had presented DNA and video evidence of Bigfoot's existence in the backwoods of Kentucky.

In 1958, workers building a road in the woods overlooking Bluff Creek in northern California were astonished to find huge footprints around their construction equipment. One of the workers, Jerry Crew, made plaster casts of some of the prints near his job site. Pictures of the 16-inch-long (40.6 cm) footprints showed up within days on the front page of the *Humboldt* (California) *Times*, and the name "Bigfoot," coined by *Times* columnist Andrew Genzoli, exploded into public usage.

The names Bigfoot and Sasquatch are both widely used today to describe a woodland creature that has 5-toed, flat feet measuring up to 27 inches (68.6 cm) long and 7 to 12 inches (17.8–30.5 cm) wide, and walks upright. Bigfoot's big toe lines up with its other four toes, unlike an ape's, which points off like a thumb, so it can be used for grasping. The prints attributed to Bigfoot don't show claws, as a bear's would.

Prints found to be several inches deep in the forest floor have meant that the creature that made them could weigh from several hundred to 1,000 pounds (455 kg). Such are the outlines the footprints have provided. People claiming to have encountered Bigfoot and even photographed him have filled in the rest of the details.

The creature could be seven to eight feet (2.1–2.4 m) tall and covered on all but its face, palms, and feet with black, brown, reddish, or even white hair. It is said that Bigfoot can scream, grunt, moan, or whoop, but most often makes a whistling sound. Its smell is distinctively awful—like rotten eggs or a dead animal. This is perhaps one reason why, in Florida, it is called the Skunk Ape. The creature is fast on its feet, too, having been clocked running alongside vehicles at 45 to 70 miles (72–113 km) per hour. Its most distinctive features, though, may be eyes that seem to glow red, pink, green, or white in the dark, not just with reflected light but at times with what appears to be their own light.

Bigfoot apparently eats just about anything: roots, berries, nuts, pine needles, and even rodents, rabbits, clams, or chickens. But where does Bigfoot sleep? How big are its babies? Can it climb trees? How long does it live? Can one Bigfoot communicate with another? Do they form communities? Do their habits change in the winter? If they resemble humans so much, why don't they seek out contact with us? No one knows.

In today's world, Bigfoot may no longer be able to avoid us. With the human population expanding, and with people finding more ways to explore and work in remote areas, Bigfoot's secret lair could be shrinking. New technology such as night-vision scopes, heat sensors, satellite-based tracking, and high-powered telescopes and sound equipment could expose

Footprint sightings by scientist Grover Krantz (opposite) and hunter Phil Thompson (above) have provided estimates of Bigfoot's size.

When a 2013 video of an ape-like animal wandering along a Canadian cliff went viral, skeptics disputed the footage.

Bigfoot more readily in its home. The Bigfoot Field Researchers Organization (BFRO) monitors and evaluates sightings, collects information and identifies **hoaxes,** and organizes expeditions to find Bigfoot while maintaining a policy that it will study Bigfoot only in ways that do the creature no harm. But the scientific community and the media alike would be riveted if anyone ever found a Bigfoot bone, not to mention an entire skeleton or skin. For those in the **documentary** film business, there's no telling how much money could be made from a movie or companion book and television show recounting that story.

Would proof of Bigfoot's existence and a detailed understanding of the creature add to or detract from its well-known reputation? Maybe neither. But a little mystery—or a lot of it—is also important, some insist. "We need to experience awe," wrote the former director of the Smithsonian Institution's **Primate** Biology Program, John Napier, in 1973. "Man needs his gods—and his monsters—and the more remote and unapproachable they are, the better."

14

Invite a Bigfoot for Dinner! Considering that Bigfoot has never left anything other than footprints behind, might it be something not quite physical? Anthropologist and author Jack Lapseritis thinks so. Lapseritis claims he has had roughly 500 visits from "Sasquatches" since 1979. He says that Sasquatches are gentle and advanced forms of humans that, although originating elsewhere in the universe, have been visiting Earth for millions of years and can communicate **telepathically** with humans. Some researchers say such ideas are so outlandish that they might have even been promoted by mining and lumber companies, which don't want Sasquatch reports taken seriously, because that might lead to wild land being closed to mining and lumbering, as a way to protect a rare species. Regardless, Lapseritis even offers some dos and don'ts for contacting the creatures:

Don't: Stalk them with weapons or cameras, or with a desire to make money off the encounter. Aggressiveness will keep them away.

Do: **Meditate**, envision a Sasquatch, and invite it to visit. Then go do something else. The Sasquatch will appear when it chooses to, Lapseritis writes.

But what about that awful smell? Lapseritis says he's never smelled it. He says Sasquatches put out the smell when they feel threatened, much like skunks.

THE
BIGFOOT
MAP

In many ways, Bigfoot ought to be an impossibility. Anthropologists believe humans have been the only **bipedal** creatures to walk exclusively upright anywhere on Earth for at least 30,000 years. If Bigfoot somehow survived as a species alongside humans for that time, why hasn't there been more evidence in the form of dens or cave sites, remains or feces? Wouldn't other animals have hunted Bigfoot and left some traces? Bigfoot evidently never mastered fire, writing, tool development, or cooking. Why not, if it supposedly has so many other human qualities? And even so, shouldn't it have left traces of a meal somewhere over the ages? Perhaps most importantly, if it lives in North America, where humans have lived for only 13,000 years, when and how did it get here?

As long as no one is sure what Bigfoot even is, it will be difficult to answer all those questions. The closest we can come is by comparing what is supposed about Bigfoot with what is known about human history. Between 5 million and 10 million years ago, some hominids in Africa began to stride on 2 feet. Why? Some scientists say that's because they needed their hands for hunting, gathering, and carrying things. In doing so, these creatures were able to live more advanced lives than their primate relatives, the apes. Their diet improved, and their brains grew because of it. Tools, fire, and speech followed. Based on the **fossil** record, other bipedal hominids developed right alongside what became modern humans, until the last of them, the **Neanderthals**, died out 30,000 to 50,000 years ago. How could one species—Bigfoot—survive, while all but one other didn't? And how could it leave no **fossils** behind?

There are other questions, of course. With the many sightings of Bigfoot on rural highways, why haven't any been killed by cars? If Bigfoot is as much ape as human, what's it doing in the Pacific Northwest, where the weather can be far colder than it is in the tropics, where apes thrive? Is that how it became so hairy, unlike humans and their relatives? Researchers have examined some hair thought to be from Bigfoot, and while they sometimes haven't been able to conclude it came from another animal, they also haven't been able to positively identify it as Bigfoot hair.

Anthropologists have long believed that humans originated in Africa and then spread across Europe and Asia. Periods of low sea levels exposed "bridges" of land that allowed early humans to cross to previously uninhabited places, such as Australia (about 60,000 years ago) and North America (much more recently, about 13,000 years ago, when the last glaciers

Scientists think gorillas (opposite) and humans split from a common ancestor about 10 million years ago and still share 96 percent of their genes.

19

retreated). Some recent findings suggest humans may have reached North America as many as 60,000 years ago, raising new questions about how and when humans got to the continent.

Those who promote Bigfoot's existence think that it came to North America the same way humans did—via a land bridge that connected the eastern tip of present-day Russia to what is now Alaska, across the Bering Sea. And Bigfoot researchers say that long before that, it might have descended from a relative that they know actually existed: *Gigantopithecus*.

In 1935, German scientist Ralph von Koenigswald was rummaging through Chinese medicine shops and bought some "dragon's teeth," fossils the Chinese would grind up into powder to make medicines. In fact, he was looking for the teeth of extinct mammals. In a Hong Kong shop, von Koenigswald found the tooth of an ape-like animal that would had to have been twice the size of a gorilla, determining that it had lived one million to 300,000 years ago. Then in 1950, Italian scientists in China found a fossilized jawbone they traced to this huge, extinct ape as well.

Only teeth and jawbones of this animal have ever been found, but those were enough to determine that it was the largest primate ever to walk the earth. *Gigantopithecus* was nearly 10 feet (3 m) tall and weighed up to 1,200 pounds (545 kg), making it far larger than the largest known ape, the 500-pound (227 kg) silverback male gorilla. It lived in northern India, China, and southeast Asia, and it is believed to have been a "knuckle-walker," like an ape. Scientists believe it may have gone extinct because humans and giant pandas may have eaten too much of its primary food, bamboo. Or, it could have wandered off in search of food and become Bigfoot.

Bigfoot is just one of many secretive "ape men" to have been sighted in remote areas around the world. Its most famous cousin is probably the yeti, thought to roam the rugged, tall peaks of the Himalaya Mountains of Tibet, Nepal, China, India, and Pakistan. The yeti is also known as the "Abominable Snowman," although the Tibetan word more accurately means "wild man of the snows."

The yeti appears in Tibetan religious art, and Tibetan monks keep what they say are yeti skins in their mountain retreats. Reports of yeti sightings are common among Sherpas, people who live in Nepal and frequently serve as guides on mountain-climbing expeditions. The first report of a yeti sighting from a European was in 1889, when a British explorer, Major L. A. Waddell, thought he spotted one in the Himalayas.

The yeti is said to be a shaggy, stooped creature that lives in caves from 12,000 to 20,000 feet (3,658–6,096 m) altitude. But, as with Bigfoot, most of the evidence is based on footprints, and a yeti's prints are not much larger than a person's. In 1951, mountaineer Eric Shipton photographed what he said was a line of prints a mile (1.6 km) long in the mountain snows. It looked **authentic**, but scientists discounted it, saying it could have been another animal's footprint that expanded as the snow melted in the intense sun. In 1960, Sir Edmund Hillary (who, along with Sherpa Tenzing Norgay, in 1953 had become the first to summit Mt. Everest), returned to the area with cameras and other gear, in part to look for yeti. They found nothing, and Hillary echoed earlier suggestions that yeti prints were those of other animals. He also famously said that the skins that Tibetan monks collected were not from yeti but from a goat known as

Pashmina goats (below), whose wool is often used for scarves, could be mistaken for the light-haired yeti of the Himalayas (opposite).

a serow and that many yeti stories and sightings might have originated with Sherpas who had embellished the tales. Some researchers have asserted that solitary footprints in snow at high altitudes in the Himalayas may have actually been made by monks walking from one valley to another. In 1995, the Chinese Academy of Sciences issued a report stating that 95 percent of yeti sightings are false and the creature does not exist. But sightings continue to be reported.

Australia also has its share of sightings of a large, reclusive, hairy figure. The yowie is reportedly nearly eight feet (2.4 m) tall with long arms and humanlike hands. Like Bigfoot, it's been described as having a repulsive body odor akin to rotting garbage or vomit. It also has glowing eyes like Bigfoot. But it is more adapted to its human neighbors, with sightings most commonly reported along the populated eastern side of the continent. In fact, it's often reported peering in windows or following people in the woods. Like Bigfoot, footprints are its only traces, but these vary in size and in form. Some are three-toed and some are five-toed.

Lakes that are frozen enough to walk on are capable of preserving trapped objects for a time, but the Minnesota Iceman was likely just a hoax.

The Father of Cryptozoology

Bernard Heuvelmans (1916–2001) was a French–Belgian scholar who earned a doctorate in zoology. But mere zoology wasn't enough to sustain his interest in the natural world. He decided to research animals that were unknown to science or thought to have gone extinct. In 1955, he published the French edition of *On the Track of Unknown Animals*, which was translated into English three years later. His work provided the foundation for an entire field he himself termed "cryptozoology," or the study of hidden animals. Heuvelmans applied traditional scientific methods but also made allowances for myths and legends, which proved popular among the general public but made the scientific community skeptical of his work. His first book sold more than one million copies. In 1968, after inspecting a creature frozen in an ice block—a former carnival exhibit—Heuvelmans declared "Minnesota Iceman" to be a type of human new to science. The Smithsonian Institution declared it a hoax. But Heuvelmans wasn't often fooled. Several years before, he had determined that what had been regarded as a piece of yeti skin was actually skin from a goat, before renowned mountaineer Sir Edmund Hillary had dismissed the yeti legend. However, in the case of the Iceman's identity, Heuvelmans later admitted his suspicions as well.

SEEING AND NOT BELIEVING

Roger Patterson's now-famous very short film of Bigfoot in action is undoubtedly the way by which most are introduced to Bigfoot—as a broad-backed, long-armed, thick-shouldered biped with a whitish face, a purposeful stride and a thick coat of lustrous dark hair that shimmers in the sun. Patterson was a former rodeo rider with such a deep interest in Bigfoot that he wrote a book in 1966 called *Do Abominable Snowmen of America Really Exist?* He was also a wildlife photographer who was working on his own documentary film about Bigfoot when, in October 1967, he and his friend Bob Gimlin went out looking for a Bigfoot. They rode into an area where there had been many sightings over the years. But what were the chances they'd actually find one, on the day they went looking with a camera?

Patterson's film is the only clear photographic image of a Bigfoot ever recorded. Patterson died only five years after making it, still insisting it was a film of a genuine Bigfoot. Gimlin also stands by the story. Krantz, the Washington State University anthropologist, has also said he believes the film to be authentic. Others say the creature's apparently muscular legs and arms are convincing.

But the film has far more detractors than supporters. Naysayers claim that the size and motion of the figure in the film make clear that it is a human in a padded ape suit. For years, it was widely believed that Hollywood makeup artist John Chambers, who won an Academy Award for designing the masks in 1968's *Planet of the Apes*, had designed the ape suit in Patterson's movie. Chambers denied it, reportedly saying he was "good but . . . not that good." Another costume-maker, Philip Morris, has told Greg Long, author of *The Making of Bigfoot: The Inside Story*, that he

Patterson's book (above) was largely criticized, but the Planet of the Apes *film franchise (opposite) has seen major box-office success.*

made the costume and sold it to Patterson, with advice on how to pad the shoulders, extend the arms, and make the head bigger by wearing a football helmet underneath. Long also interviewed a friend of Patterson's, Bob Hieronimous, who well after Patterson's death claimed that he had worn the suit and played Bigfoot in Patterson's film. The suit has never been found.

The tracks Bigfoot left behind that day were 41 inches (104 cm) apart, which would be a very long stride for a person. Researchers have pointed out that if the Patterson film was shot at a slow speed, the figure would have to have taken long strides at a slow speed and make it look easy. But that would not be simple for a 6-foot-tall (1.8 m) person to do, and that was the size of the Bigfoot in Patterson's film (which is small for a Bigfoot). However, if the film was shot at a faster-than-normal speed, the stride might be accomplished by a person. So if the camera was running fast, the figure in the movie could very likely be a person in a costume. If it was running slow, it might have been something else. The problem is that no one knows the speed at which Patterson's camera was running.

Although the Patterson film has understandably given a widely accepted identity to Bigfoot, there have been hundreds of other descriptions through the years of an elusive woodland creature believed to be Bigfoot.

In 1892, Theodore Roosevelt, who became the 26th U.S. president in 1901, wrote *The Wilderness Hunter*, in which he repeated the story of a young fur trapper and his partner who were stalked in the woods by a smelly, two-legged creature. Each day, when they returned from checking and setting traps, they would find their camp destroyed. One night, the trapper, a man named Baumann, heard a commotion outside his tent and fired his shotgun toward the noise. Whatever it was ran off. The next day, when Baumann came back from checking traps, he found his partner dead with a broken neck.

Another story involved five miners in a cabin on Washington's Mount St. Helens in 1924. One day one of the miners saw a Bigfoot and fired at it. That night, their cabin was attacked by several Bigfoot, one of which even punched through the wall. The attack lasted five hours. Although that story, too, was later dismissed, it caused enough excitement at the time that the area was named Ape Canyon.

That same year—although nobody at the time connected the stories—a logger named Albert Ostman, who was searching for gold while vacationing in British Columbia, was carried and dragged for three hours in his sleeping bag, unable to reach his knife to cut himself free. At dawn he found himself in a camp with a family of Bigfoot—what appeared to be a father, a mother, a young male, and a young female. Ostman was closely watched for six days until he offered the 8-foot-tall (2.4 m) adult male Bigfoot his tin of tobacco. The Bigfoot ate it and, either sick or disgusted, ran off to a creek for a drink. That's when Ostman escaped, firing a shot back at the adult female.

Although researchers such as John Napier remained unconvinced by the tobacco story, Ostman swore under oath it was the truth.

Ostman didn't tell his story for 37 years, so no one looked for evidence. He said he thought no one would believe him. Some say that because he waited until other stories started emerging, in the late 1950s, his story isn't credible. Others say that the fact he recalled so much detail, including how he was first lifted at 4:25 A.M. (he had been able to look at his watch while being carried), makes it more plausible.

Some researchers note that the older stories of Bigfoot encounters portray the creature as an aggressive monster. In 1941, for instance, a British Columbia family was chased from their home by a Bigfoot they first thought was a bear, but which later ransacked their home. More recent reports, however, describe only fleeting glimpses or footprints, suggesting an apparently shy creature. And while it seems that someone often claims to have staged the encounters as a practical joke—using a costume, or huge carved feet to make prints—some scholars argue that the sheer number of reported sightings means that they can't all be fake. Even some of the **debunked** ones might prove to be authentic.

The family of Ray Wallace, the foreman on the 1958 Bluff Creek road crew that found footprints that led to the label "Bigfoot," said after Wallace died that he had made the prints from wooden blocks. But a fingerprint expert later said the prints showed patterns that indicated they'd been made by an unknown species of primate. In 1969, some huge footprints found near Bossburg, Washington, attracted a spotlight, even though they were found by an amateur naturalist with a reputation as a practical joker who had just moved to the area. However, the Smithsonian's Napier and anthropologist Krantz both said it was unlikely that a footprint like that could have been faked.

"It is very difficult to conceive of a hoaxer so subtle, so knowledge-able—and so sick—who would deliberately fake a footprint of this nature," Napier wrote. "I suppose it is possible, but it is so unlikely that I am prepared to discount it."

Sasquatch hands are believed to be similar to those of orangutans (below) and humans, with four long fingers and an opposable thumb.

The sightings have continued, however. The BFRO posted more than 100 "new" sightings that it regarded as credible on its website from February through mid-May 2013. Many of those sightings were from years ago and based on memory, but the BFRO promises full and complete investigation into all of them.

Bigfoot: This Exit Bigfoot is known as a shadowy creature who lives deep in the woods where it's rarely seen. But it's a familiar and big attraction in Willow Creek, California, a place nicknamed "The Gateway to Bigfoot Country." Willow Creek is a town of approximately 2,000 people in northwestern California along the Klamath River and about 20 miles (32.2 km) south of Bluff Creek, where the famous footprints were sighted in 1958. Bigfoot has left a mark on the city bigger than any footprints. Several carved statues keep watch over the comings and goings of townspeople and tourists. One stands at the turn to the Bigfoot Scenic Byway, an 89-mile (143 km) road through the Salmon Mountains that is regarded as prime Bigfoot country. There's a Bigfoot Motel, a Bigfoot Golf and Country Club, and Bigfoot Books, but the main attraction for Bigfoot seekers may be the Bigfoot Museum, guarded by another gigantic statue. The museum has a collection of photos, footprint casts, press clippings, maps, and, of course, souvenir T-shirts. It regards itself as a Bigfoot research center. But the Bigfoot legend is big enough to support competition. The Bigfoot Discovery Museum is located south of San Francisco, California.

BIGFOOT: AN

OPEN OR CLOSED CASE?

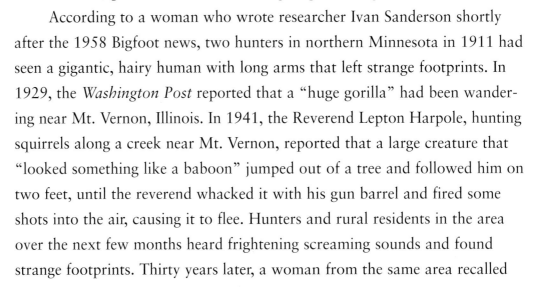

Bigfoot is clearly one of the most elusive creatures on Earth, especially considering its purported size. Its run-ins with humans, while often startling, have been few and far between. It could be that there simply aren't many Bigfoot around, that the species is on its way to extinction, or both. That might make it not just elusive but possibly lonely as well.

Yet it seems Bigfoot might have cousins in a larger family of similar unusual North American creatures. The *Encyclopedia of Strange and Unexplained Physical Phenomena* has an all-inclusive term for these animals: "hairy bipeds." These are creatures that have been reported far from Bigfoot's home country, in regular and numerous encounters over the decades long before Bigfoot was named, defined, and precisely located in 1958. They have usually been sighted in rural areas and showed some Bigfoot characteristics but not all. Most have been tall, but some have been short. Some have had glowing eyes. Some, three toes. Some, three legs. And in some cases, gunshots have seemed to go right through them.

According to a woman who wrote researcher Ivan Sanderson shortly after the 1958 Bigfoot news, two hunters in northern Minnesota in 1911 had seen a gigantic, hairy human with long arms that left strange footprints. In 1929, the *Washington Post* reported that a "huge gorilla" had been wandering near Mt. Vernon, Illinois. In 1941, the Reverend Lepton Harpole, hunting squirrels along a creek near Mt. Vernon, reported that a large creature that "looked something like a baboon" jumped out of a tree and followed him on two feet, until the reverend whacked it with his gun barrel and fired some shots into the air, causing it to flee. Hunters and rural residents in the area over the next few months heard frightening screaming sounds and found strange footprints. Thirty years later, a woman from the same area recalled

On a plentiful diet of small woodland mammals, plants, and berries, the lone Bigfoot could easily survive in the western wilderness.

that her two brothers, when they were boys in the early part of the 20th century, occasionally saw hairy creatures that stood on their hind legs, had large eyes, and were about the size of a person or perhaps shorter. They seemed harmless, though.

Modern America is regarded as more skeptical and less superstitious than it was in the 19th century and the first half of the 20th, as urbanization and more forms of communication have helped people share ideas more readily. But reports of encounters with hairy bipeds, if anything, have become more regular.

Among the scenarios:

• Christine Van Acker, a 17-year-old girl from Monroe, Michigan, got a black eye on August 11, 1965, after a 7-foot-tall (2.1 m) hairy giant stepped into the road in front of the car her mother was driving, approached the car, reached in, and grabbed the girl. The girl screamed, and nearby workers responded as the creature retreated.

• George Kaiser, a farmer near Rising Sun, Indiana, in 1969 watched a 5-foot-8 (1.7 m) hairy creature with humanlike hands for about 2 minutes at a distance of about 25 feet (7.6 m) before it ran off, leaving large, 4-toed prints behind.

• Randy and Lou Rogers were visited by a large hairy "gorilla" at their home outside Roachdale, Indiana, several times in the summer of 1972. It ran on all fours, but Lou Rogers said it never left tracks. A nearby farmer claimed it ripped apart nearly 200 of his chickens, and though his uncle shot at it several times at close range, it escaped apparently unharmed.

• Noxie, Oklahoma, farmer Kenneth Tosh and his neighbors in 1975 reported seeing a pair of hairy creatures with glowing eyes that both stood more than 6 feet (1.8 m) tall, screaming and smelling like rotten eggs.

• Between 1977 and 1993, people in Tuscola County, Michigan, reported encounters with hairy bipeds on farms and roads 38 different times. That's more than two sightings per year.

• Through the 1990s and 2000s, campers, drivers, forest workers, and others—some searching for Bigfoot, others caught completely by surprise—have filed numerous reports of piercing sounds at night; sightings of big, hairy, two-legged creatures crossing roads; and even face-to-face encounters.

Most scientists don't have the time, money, or patience to pursue a

Bigfoot supporters believe tabloids, or magazines, featuring tales of the creature kidnapping people or wreaking havoc are harmfully misleading.

mystery, whether it involves animals, planets, cells, or even invisible forces, unless there is ample evidence that it can be examined in the first place. They want something they can measure or put under a microscope. They want bones or fur for a clear picture. They want something that exists.

Think about dinosaurs. Even though no human has ever seen a *Tyrannosaurus rex*, we know pretty well that it was a meat-eating lizard with an enormous head balanced by an enormous tail. We know that it walked on two heavy legs and had two tiny arms with claws for grasping other animals it was about to chomp on with its mouthful of teeth. We know that it was one of the largest carnivores (meat-eaters) ever to roam the earth. And we know this because it left so many bones behind. From them, scientists have been able to reconstruct complete skeletons that now stand, life-sized and fully reassembled, in museums around the world. They've also been able to determine much about how the dinosaur lived.

But Bigfoot is another matter. Somehow, a creature that some believe has lived alongside humans for tens of thousands of years hasn't left a single bone behind, despite living a challenging life in the wilderness. Does it simply vanish when it dies—bones, hair, and all? It's possible, since Bigfoot is rare in the first place. But it's also unlikely, and one reason why many scientists don't take Bigfoot stories seriously.

Some say that Bigfoot and hairy bipeds are products of the many ways humans can interpret (or misinterpret) the things they see, hear, smell, and feel, or mix reality with explanations of the unknown and unusual. That's likely how humans came up with the satyrs, cyclops, dragons, and other mythological creatures. Likewise, author and skeptic Greg Long says that the humanlike Bigfoot illustrates modern North Americans' emotional need to

Considering that remains of the prehistoric T. rex were not discovered until the late 1800s, some think proof of Bigfoot is simply yet to be found.

Dr. Jane Goodall spent decades studying wild chimpanzees and discovered their social behaviors, communication, and use of tools.

remain connected to wild things in the face of increasing mechanization. But others say: Hold on.

Dr. Jeff Meldrum, associate professor of anatomy and anthropology at Idaho State University, who paid little attention to Bigfoot until he came across some fresh tracks in 1996, thinks scientists aren't giving enough weight to eyewitness accounts of Bigfoot. And that, he writes in his book *Sasquatch: Legend Meets Science*, means they might be missing a good story. Finding and documenting Bigfoot, he writes, "may eventually prove to be among the most astounding zoological discoveries ever."

Dr. Jane Goodall, a primatologist who is regarded as the world's expert on chimpanzees, also says that centuries of Bigfoot-like tales among various

American Indian cultures is a form of validation that it is out there. "There remains a species of great ape to be discovered," she said in a 2002 radio interview. "I'm sure they exist."

Napier, the Smithsonian scholar, wrote that Bigfoot sightings are easy to dismiss, since so many have been hoaxes. "But if any one of them is real, then as scientists we have a lot to explain," he wrote. "We shall have to admit that there are still major mysteries to be solved in a world we thought we knew so well."

Will Bigfoot ever truly reveal itself? Or will humans have to find it? In either case, the quest to solve the mysteries is one that is certain to teach us much about ourselves.

Don't Shoot! If Bigfoot is worried about being hunted, it could rest easier in the woods of Skamania County, Washington. In 1969, county commissioners passed a law making it illegal to kill a Bigfoot. They acknowledged that both legend and "recent sightings and spoor" supported the possibility that Bigfoot was roaming in southwestern Washington, near Portland, Oregon. They added that publicity about Bigfoot had drawn so many people with guns into the woods, without any kind of regulated hunt, that a ban was needed to protect "the safety and well-being of persons living or traveling within the boundaries of Skamania County as well as . . . the creatures themselves." The ordinance was passed on April 1, making some people think it was a joke. But it was later amended to make shooting a Bigfoot a **homicide**, which also made Bigfoot the legal equivalent of a human being. In the state's northwestern corner, Whatcom County, along the Canadian border north of Seattle, declared itself in 1992 to be a "Sasquatch Protection and Refuge Area." However, hunting officials in states such as Texas have said that as long as Bigfoot is not known to science, not classified as being endangered, and not mentioned in hunting laws, people can hunt it any time.

Field Notes

authentic: undisputed, based on facts, accurate

bipedal: walking on two feet

casts: reproductions or impressions of objects or images, often made with plaster

debunked: proven false

documentary: a film, television program, or similar work that presents factual subject matter such as history or science

fossil: the remains or impression of ancient plants or animals preserved in rock

hoaxes: humorous or harmful deceptions; tricks

homicide: murder; the deliberate killing of a person

hominid: human or related humanlike creatures, including other primates such as apes, orangutans, and chimpanzees

meditate: to think deeply or concentrate on an idea, sound, or image in order to clear one's mind of distractions

myth: a traditional story that tries to explain how something came to be or involves people or things with exaggerated qualities

Neanderthals: the latest-surviving hominid relative of modern humans known, which lived in Europe and Asia and died out about 30,000 years ago

primate: a member of an order of mammals that includes humans, monkeys, apes, and lemurs, among others

spoor: a footprint, track, or scent of an animal

telepathically: using a means of communication other than the known physical senses

Selected Bibliography

Clark, Jerome. *Encyclopedia of Strange and Unexplained Physical Phenomena.* Detroit, Mich.: Gale Research, 1993.

Emmer, Rick. *Bigfoot: Fact or Fiction?* New York: Chelsea House, 2010.

Krensky, Stephen. *Bigfoot.* Minneapolis: Lerner Publications, 2007.

Lapseritis, Jack. *The Psychic Sasquatch and their UFO Connection.* Mill Spring, N.C.: Blue Water Publishing, 1998.

Meldrum, Jeff. *Sasquatch: Legend Meets Science.* New York: Tom Doherty Associates, 2006.

Napier, John. *Bigfoot: The Yeti and Sasquatch in Myth and Reality.* New York: Dutton, 1973.

Sanderson, Ivan T. *Abominable Snowmen: Legend Come to Life.* Philadelphia: Chilton, 1961.

Worth, Bonnie. *Looking for Bigfoot.* New York: Random House, 2010.

Websites

BIGFOOT FIELD RESEARCHERS ORGANIZATION
http://www.bfro.net/
This site features interactive maps, sighting documentation, research, photos, and sound recordings.

BIGFOOT-LIVES.COM
http://www.bigfoot-lives.com/html/bigfoot_video_and_audio.html
Bigfoot films (including the Patterson film), interviews with researchers, and discussions of hoaxes are presented.

Note: *Every effort has been made to ensure that the websites listed above are suitable for children, that they have educational value, and that they contain no inappropriate material. However, because of the nature of the Internet, it is impossible to guarantee that these sites will remain active indefinitely or that their contents will not be altered.*

Index